Mastering Financial Planning.

Unlock Your Financial Potential: Discover, Plan, and Prosper!

Robert Lewis

Cover design by Becca Barnard

Barnard Publishing Ltd
Wales

barnard.publishing@gmail.com

www.barnardpublishing.co.uk

Mastering Financial Planning

Introduction from the Author

As a financial adviser and co-founder of a firm of independent financial advisers, I have dedicated my career to helping individuals and families navigate the often complex world of financial planning, an occupation I have come to love. Over the years, I have witnessed first-hand the profound impact that sound financial advice and planning can have on the lives of countless families. I've seen people achieve their dreams of home-ownership, secure a comfortable retirement, and create lasting legacies for their loved ones, all because they had the right guidance and tools to make informed decisions.

My passion for good financial planning and the desire to empower more people with the knowledge and resources to improve their financial lives have been the driving forces behind the creation of this book. I believe that everyone, regardless of their financial background or level of expertise, should have access to the same high-quality advice and insights that my clients receive. This book is my attempt to bridge that gap and serve as a comprehensive guide to help readers make sound financial decisions that align with their values, goals, and personal circumstances.

Through the chapters of this book, I aim to provide a roadmap for navigating the various aspects of financial planning, from understanding the role of regulatory bodies like the FCA and PRA to building a well-diversified investment portfolio and planning for life's milestones. Drawing on my years of experience as an independent financial adviser, I offer practical advice, real-life examples, and useful resources to help readers gain a better understanding of the complex financial landscape.

My hope is that this book serves as a trusted companion on your journey towards financial freedom and success. By sharing my knowledge and experience, I hope to inspire you to take charge of your financial future, make informed decisions, and ultimately, improve the financial lives of you and your family.

Wishing you every success on your financial journey,

Robert Lewis
Co-founder and Independent Financial Adviser

Risk Warning and Disclaimer: The information contained in this book is provided for general informational purposes only and should not be construed as financial advice. The content is intended to serve as a guide to help readers understand various aspects of financial planning and investing but should not be relied upon as the sole basis for making financial decisions. Readers should consult their own tax, legal, and financial advisers before making any investment or financial planning decisions. The author and publisher are not responsible for any errors or omissions or for the results obtained from the use of this information. All investments carry risks, including the potential loss of capital, and past performance is not indicative of future results.

Chapter 1: Introduction

1.1 The Importance of Financial Planning

Financial planning is a critical aspect of personal finance, as it involves the process of setting financial goals, managing resources, and creating a roadmap to achieve financial stability and long-term wealth. It provides a structured approach to managing your money, allowing you to make informed decisions about saving, investing, and spending.

- Effective financial planning enables you to:
- Achieve your short-term and long-term financial goals
- Build a solid financial foundation to weather economic storms
- Make well-informed decisions to grow and protect your wealth
- Provide financial security for you and your family
- Reduce financial stress and enjoy a better quality of life
- Retire comfortably and leave a lasting legacy

By taking the time to create a comprehensive financial plan, you equip yourself with the tools and knowledge needed to navigate the complex world of personal finance and investing.

This book serves as a guide to cover a number of areas of financial planning, you can pick up a chapter in isolation to learn more about that topic. However, it should not be seen as financial advice. I would always recommend the services of a good independent financial adviser.

1.2 The UK Financial Landscape

The United Kingdom, being one of the world's leading financial centres, offers a wide range of opportunities and resources for investors. Understanding the unique aspects of the UK financial landscape is essential for investors seeking to make the most of their money and build wealth in the country.

Key elements of the UK financial landscape include:

- Currency: The official currency of the UK is the British Pound Sterling (GBP). This currency is widely accepted and can be easily converted to other currencies when needed.
- Central Bank: The Bank of England serves as the UK's central bank and is responsible for setting monetary policy, maintaining financial stability, and regulating the country's banking system.
- Taxation: The UK operates a progressive income tax system, with rates varying based on income levels. Capital gains tax, inheritance tax, and other taxes also play a role in shaping the financial landscape for investors.
- Regulatory Bodies: The Financial Conduct Authority (FCA) and the Prudential Regulation Authority (PRA) are the main regulatory bodies overseeing the financial services industry in the UK. These organisations ensure that financial institutions adhere to regulations and protect consumers.
- Investment Vehicles: UK investors have access to a diverse range of investment options, including stocks, bonds, mutual funds, exchange-traded funds (ETFs), property, and alternative investments. Tax-efficient vehicles, such as Individual Savings Accounts (ISAs) and pensions, provide additional opportunities for building wealth.

Understanding these elements and staying up to date with changes in the financial landscape will help UK investors make informed decisions and maximise their financial success.

1.2.1 The Financial Conduct Authority (FCA)

The Financial Conduct Authority (FCA) is an independent regulatory body responsible for supervising and regulating the financial services industry in the United Kingdom. Established in 2013, the FCA took over the responsibilities of the Financial Services Authority (FSA) and is funded by fees charged to the firms it regulates. The FCA's primary objectives are to protect consumers, maintain the integrity of the UK financial system, and promote competition in the interest of consumers.

The FCA regulates financial planning by:

0.1. Setting standards: The FCA establishes rules and guidelines that financial advisors and planners must follow, ensuring they adhere to ethical and professional standards.

0.2. Licensing: Financial advisors and planners are required to obtain appropriate qualifications and maintain their knowledge through continuing professional development (CPD). The FCA monitors their compliance and has the power to revoke licenses if necessary.

0.3. Supervision: The FCA monitors the activities of financial planning firms and conducts regular assessments to ensure they are operating in compliance with regulations.

0.4. Enforcement: The FCA has the authority to take enforcement action against firms and individuals that breach regulations, which can include fines, penalties, and even criminal prosecutions.

1.2.2 The Prudential Regulation Authority (PRA)

The Prudential Regulation Authority (PRA) is another key regulatory body in the UK financial landscape. Established alongside the FCA in 2013, the PRA is a part of the Bank of England and is responsible for the prudential regulation and supervision of banks, building societies, credit unions, insurers, and major investment firms. Its primary objective is to ensure the stability of the UK financial system by promoting the safety and soundness of regulated firms.

While the PRA does not have a direct role in regulating financial planning, its oversight of financial institutions helps to create a stable environment for financial planning firms and their clients.

1.2.3 The Financial Services Compensation Scheme (FSCS)

The Financial Services Compensation Scheme (FSCS) is the UK's statutory compensation fund for customers of financial services firms authorised by the FCA and PRA. Established in 2001, the FSCS provides a safety net for consumers in case a regulated financial services firm is unable to meet its financial obligations or goes out of business.

The FSCS covers various financial products and services, including deposits, insurance policies, investments, and pensions. The compensation limits for different types of products and services may vary. For example, the FSCS offers up to £85,000 per person, per institution for deposits, and up to £85,000 per person for investments.

By regulating financial planning and providing compensation through the FSCS, the FCA and PRA offer a level of assurance to consumers that their money is protected when dealing with regulated financial services firms. It is essential for investors to ensure they work with financial planners and advisors who are authorised by the FCA to benefit from these protections.

1.3. Why use a Financial Adviser

In today's increasingly complex financial landscape, the value of professional advice cannot be underestimated. A financial adviser can be a valuable resource, providing expert guidance and support to help you navigate the world of personal finance and make well-informed decisions that align with your financial goals. In this insert, we'll explore the benefits of using a financial adviser and discuss some compelling statistics that highlight the positive impact of professional advice on your financial life.

- Personalised Financial Plans: Financial advisers work closely with clients to create tailored financial plans that take into account individual needs, goals, and risk tolerance. This personalised approach ensures that your financial plan is aligned with your unique circumstances, helping you to achieve your objectives more efficiently and effectively.

- Expertise and Knowledge: Financial advisers are highly skilled professionals with extensive knowledge of various financial products, investment strategies, and regulatory requirements. This expertise allows them to recommend suitable investment options, minimise tax liabilities, and ensure that your financial plan is compliant with relevant regulations.

- Long-term Perspective: A financial adviser can help you maintain a long-term perspective when it comes to your finances, ensuring that your decisions are guided by your overarching financial objectives rather than short-term market fluctuations.

- Behavioural Coaching: Financial advisers can also act as behavioural coaches, helping you to avoid common psychological pitfalls that can negatively impact your investment returns. By providing objective guidance and support, they can help you to maintain discipline and stay on track with your financial plan, even during challenging market conditions.
- Time Savings: Managing your finances can be time-consuming and complex, particularly when it comes to researching investment options and keeping up-to-date with regulatory changes. A financial adviser can take on this responsibility, freeing up your time to focus on other important aspects of your life.

According to a study by Vanguard, investors who work with a financial adviser can experience additional net returns of about 3% on average, primarily due to the benefits of personalised advice, behavioural coaching, and cost-effective investment strategies (Source: Vanguard, "Advisor's Alpha," 2019). Furthermore, a report by the International Longevity Centre-UK (ILC-UK) found that individuals who received professional financial advice between 2001-2007 accumulated, on average, £41,099 more in pension wealth by 2012-2014 than those who did not receive advice (Source: ILC-UK, "The Value of Financial Advice," 2017).

These statistics underscore the significant benefits that financial advisers can bring to your financial life, helping you to make more informed decisions and maximise your wealth over time. By working with a financial adviser, you can gain valuable insights, expert guidance, and the peace of mind that comes from knowing that your financial future is in capable hands.

1.4 Independent vs Restricted Financial Advice

When seeking financial advice, it's important to understand the difference between independent and restricted financial advice. Both types of advice can offer valuable insights and guidance, but they differ in terms of the range of products and services they can recommend.

Independent Financial Advice:

- Independent financial advisors (IFAs) can consider and recommend financial products from across the entire market, without any limitations or biases towards specific providers or product types. This means that they can offer a broader range of options and tailor their recommendations to your unique financial needs and circumstances. The benefits of independent financial advice include:
- Unbiased recommendations: IFAs have no allegiance to specific financial institutions, ensuring that their advice is objective and solely focused on your best interests.
- Comprehensive product selection: As independent advisors can access the entire market, they can identify the most suitable financial products and strategies for your specific needs.
- Customised advice: Independent advisors can provide personalised guidance based on your unique financial goals, risk tolerance, and circumstances.
- Holistic financial planning: Many independent advisors offer comprehensive financial planning services, addressing multiple aspects of your financial life, such as investments, retirement planning, tax planning, and estate planning.

Restricted Financial Advice:

Restricted financial advisors, on the other hand, can only recommend a limited range of financial products or services, typically those provided by a specific financial institution or a limited selection of providers. This type of advice may be suitable if you are seeking guidance on specific products or services offered by a particular provider. However, restricted advisors may not be able to provide the same level of unbiased, comprehensive advice as independent advisors.

In conclusion, the primary difference between independent and restricted financial advice lies in the scope of products and services they can recommend. Independent financial advice offers the benefit of unbiased, comprehensive, and personalised guidance tailored to your unique financial needs. When selecting a financial advisor, it's essential to consider the type of advice that best suits your financial objectives and preferences.

In this book, we will guide you through the essential aspects of financial planning tailored to the UK market. From setting goals and understanding risk tolerance to navigating the various investment options and tax-efficient strategies, you will learn how to master your money and build wealth in the United Kingdom.

Chapter 2: Establishing Your Financial Goals

2.1 Short-term vs. Long-term Goals

Before diving into the world of financial planning, it is essential to have a clear understanding of your financial goals. These goals serve as the foundation of your financial plan and help you determine the strategies and investment vehicles that are best suited to achieve them. Financial goals can be broadly categorised into short-term and long-term goals:

- Short-term goals: These are financial objectives that you aim to achieve within the next one to five years. Examples of short-term goals include saving for a vacation, purchasing a car, or building an emergency fund.
- Long-term goals: These are financial objectives that you aim to achieve over an extended period, typically more than five years. Examples of long-term goals include saving for a child's education, buying a home, or planning for retirement.

It is crucial to strike a balance between short-term and long-term goals to ensure you are prepared for immediate needs while also planning for the future.

2.2 SMART Goals for Investors

Setting financial goals can be a daunting task, especially when you consider the multitude of factors that can influence your financial situation. To simplify the process and increase the likelihood of success, it is helpful to use the SMART criteria when defining your financial goals. SMART stands for Specific, Measurable, Achievable, Relevant, and Time-bound:

- Specific: Clearly define your financial goals, outlining the exact outcome you desire. For example, instead of stating, "I want to save for a new car," specify the make and model of the car and the amount you need to save.
- Measurable: Ensure your financial goals can be tracked and measured. This allows you to monitor your progress and adjust your strategies as needed. For example, if your goal is to save £20,000 for a home deposit, set milestones along the

way, such as saving £5,000 each year.

- Achievable: Your financial goals should be realistic and attainable based on your income, expenses, and financial resources. Setting overly ambitious goals may lead to disappointment and frustration.
- Relevant: Your financial goals should align with your values, priorities, and overall financial plan. For example, if you are focused on saving for retirement, it may not be the best time to plan for an expensive vacation.
- Time-bound: Assign a deadline to your financial goals to create a sense of urgency and motivation. For example, if your goal is to save £10,000 for an emergency fund, set a specific date by which you want to achieve this goal, such as within two years.

By establishing SMART financial goals, you create a clear and actionable roadmap that guides your financial planning efforts and increases your chances of success.

2.3 Prioritising Goals & Needs

A crucial aspect of effective financial planning is prioritising your goals and needs. Having a clear understanding of your short-term and long-term financial objectives will help guide your financial decisions and ensure that you stay on track towards achieving those goals.

To prioritise your financial goals and needs, consider the following steps:

0.1. List your financial goals: Begin by identifying all the financial goals you want to achieve, both in the short term (e.g., paying off credit card debt) and long term (e.g., saving for retirement).

0.2. Categorise your goals: Divide your goals into three categories - needs, wants, and aspirations. Needs are essentials that you must address for your financial well-being (e.g., paying off high-interest debt), wants are important but not critical (e.g., buying a new car), and aspirations are long-term dreams that can be pursued once other priorities are met (e.g., taking a dream vacation).

0.3. Determine the time frame: For each goal, establish a realistic time frame for achieving it. This will help you develop a more accurate plan for allocating your resources and give you a better sense of the urgency of each goal.

0.4. Assess the resources required: Estimate the financial resources required to achieve each goal, considering factors such as current savings, investment returns, and potential future income.

0.5. Rank your goals: Based on the importance, time frame, and resources required, rank your goals in order of priority. This will help you focus on what is most important and allocate your resources accordingly.

0.6. Review and adjust: Periodically reassess your goals and their priority, as life events or changes in your financial situation may require you to re-evaluate your objectives and the resources available to achieve them.

By prioritising your financial goals and needs, you can develop a more focused and effective financial plan that aligns with your values and helps you achieve your desired financial outcomes. Remember, establishing clear priorities is key to making informed decisions and staying on track towards your financial goals.

In this chapter, we have explored the importance of setting short-term and long-term financial goals and using the SMART criteria to define them effectively. In the following chapters, we will delve deeper into various aspects of financial planning and investment strategies to help you achieve these goals and build a strong financial future in the UK.

Chapter 3: Understanding Your Risk Tolerance

3.1 The Importance of Risk Tolerance

Risk tolerance is a critical factor in financial planning and investing, as it determines your ability and willingness to cope with fluctuations in the value of your investments. Understanding your risk tolerance allows you to make informed decisions about your investment strategy, ensuring that you select an appropriate mix of assets that align with your financial goals and comfort level.

There are generally three categories of risk tolerance:

0.1. Conservative: Investors with a conservative risk tolerance prefer stability and are unwilling to accept significant fluctuations in their investments. They prioritise capital preservation over potential high returns and typically choose low-risk investments such as government bonds, fixed-income securities, and cash equivalents.

0.2. Moderate: Investors with a moderate risk tolerance are willing to accept some fluctuations in the value of their investments in exchange for potentially higher returns. They often opt for a balanced mix of low-risk and higher-risk assets, such as a combination of bonds and stocks.

0.3. Aggressive: Investors with an aggressive risk tolerance prioritise high returns and are willing to accept substantial fluctuations in their investments. They typically choose high-risk assets such as stocks, high-yield bonds, and alternative investments.

3.2 Risk Assessment Tools

Several risk assessment tools are available to help you determine your risk tolerance, including online questionnaires, financial advisors, and self-assessment techniques. These tools typically consider factors such as your age, income, investment goals, financial knowledge, and investment experience to gauge your risk tolerance.

- Online questionnaires: Numerous websites and investment platforms offer risk tolerance questionnaires that ask a series of questions related to your financial situation, investment objectives, and personal preferences. These questionnaires typically provide a risk tolerance score, which can guide your investment strategy.

- Financial advisors: A professional financial advisor can assess your risk tolerance by considering your financial goals, resources, and personal circumstances. They can also help you understand the implications of different risk levels and recommend an investment strategy that suits your risk tolerance.
- Self-assessment: Reflecting on your financial goals, investment history, and your reactions to past market fluctuations can provide valuable insight into your risk tolerance. Consider how you would feel if the value of your investments dropped significantly and whether you would be able to maintain a long-term perspective during turbulent times.

3.3 Balancing Risk and Reward

An essential aspect of financial planning is balancing risk and reward to achieve your financial goals while remaining within your comfort zone. Historically, investments with higher risk potential, such as stocks, have generated higher returns over the long term compared to low-risk assets like bonds and cash. However, these higher returns come with increased volatility and the possibility of short-term losses.

A well-diversified portfolio that includes a mix of asset classes can help you balance risk and reward while aligning with your risk tolerance. Diversification reduces the impact of any single investment on your portfolio, allowing you to spread risk across various investments and achieve more stable returns.

According to a study by Vanguard, a diversified portfolio containing 60% stocks and 40% bonds has historically provided an average annual return of 8.3%, with a standard deviation (a measure of volatility) of 11.2%. In contrast, a portfolio containing 100% stocks had an average annual return of 10.2%, but with a higher standard deviation of 18.7%.

3.4 Capacity for loss

In the context of investing, capacity for loss refers to an investor's ability to withstand financial losses without jeopardising their financial security or lifestyle. It is a crucial factor to consider when building an investment portfolio, as it helps ensure that you do not take on more risk than you can comfortably afford.

Your capacity for loss can be influenced by various factors, including:

- Financial resources: An investor with a higher net worth, steady income, and a well-funded emergency fund may have a greater capacity for loss compared to someone with fewer financial resources or less stable income.
- Time horizon: The length of time until you need to access your investments can impact your capacity for loss. If you have a longer time horizon, you may be better positioned to ride out market fluctuations and recover from potential losses. Conversely, a shorter time horizon may require a more conservative approach, as you have less time to recover from any losses.
- Financial goals: Your capacity for loss can also depend on the importance and urgency of your financial goals. If you are investing for a critical goal, such as funding your child's education or your retirement, you may have a lower capacity for loss compared to someone investing for a more flexible goal, such as a vacation or home improvement project.
- Emotional tolerance for loss: Your psychological ability to handle financial losses is another aspect of your capacity for loss. Some investors may be more emotionally resilient and better able to tolerate market volatility, while others may become anxious or stressed by even minor losses.

To assess your capacity for loss, consider your financial situation, investment goals, and emotional responses to risk. Once you have a clear understanding of your capacity for loss, you can make informed decisions about your asset allocation and investment strategy, ensuring that you do not take on more risk than you can comfortably manage. Remember that investing always involves some degree of risk, and it's essential to strike a balance between pursuing your financial goals and protecting your financial well-being.

Personal Tip: Be honest with yourself about your risk tolerance. Remember that investing always involves some level of risk, but it's crucial to strike a balance between potential rewards and the risks you're comfortable taking.

In this chapter, we have discussed the importance of understanding your risk tolerance and the tools available to assess it. As you progress through the book, you will learn more about various investment strategies and asset classes, enabling you to make informed decisions that align with your risk tolerance and financial goals.

Chapter 4: Building a Solid Financial Foundation

Before delving into investment strategies and portfolio construction, it is vital to establish a strong financial foundation. This foundation will provide you with financial security and stability, allowing you to confidently navigate the world of investing.

4.1 Emergency Funds

An emergency fund is a crucial component of a solid financial foundation. It serves as a financial safety net, providing you with readily available funds to cover unexpected expenses or income loss without resorting to high-interest debt.

Financial experts typically recommend having three to six months' worth of living expenses saved in an emergency fund. This amount may vary depending on factors such as job stability, number of income sources, and individual circumstances.

To build an emergency fund:

0.1. Determine the amount needed to cover your living expenses for the desired period.

0.2. Set up a separate savings account specifically for your emergency fund.

0.3. Allocate a portion of your monthly income to your emergency fund until you reach your target amount.

4.2 Insurance and Protection

Insurance plays a critical role in protecting your financial well-being and that of your family. It can provide financial support during difficult times, such as illness, injury, or the loss of a loved one. Key insurance policies to consider include:

- Life insurance: Provides financial support to your dependants in the event of your death, helping to cover living expenses, debts, and future financial needs.
- Health insurance: Covers medical expenses, enabling you to receive the necessary care without incurring significant out-of-pocket costs.

- Income protection insurance: Provides a regular income if you are unable to work due to illness or injury, ensuring you can continue to meet your financial obligations.
- Home insurance: Protects your property and belongings against damage or loss due to events such as theft, fire, or natural disasters.

Evaluate your insurance needs based on your personal circumstances and financial responsibilities, and review your coverage periodically to ensure it remains adequate.

4.3 Wills and Estate Planning

Estate planning is the process of organising your financial affairs and determining how your assets will be distributed upon your death. A well-crafted estate plan can provide peace of mind, reduce potential tax liabilities, and ensure that your loved ones are taken care of according to your wishes.

Key components of estate planning include:

0.1. Creating a will: A will is a legal document that outlines how your assets will be distributed upon your death. It allows you to designate beneficiaries, appoint an executor, and provide specific instructions for the distribution of your estate.

0.2. Designating beneficiaries: Ensure that your financial accounts, insurance policies, and retirement plans have up-to-date beneficiary designations, as these typically supersede instructions in your will.

0.3. Establishing trusts: Trusts can be an effective estate planning tool, providing tax benefits and allowing you to maintain control over how your assets are managed and distributed.

0.4. Lasting power of attorney (LPA): An LPA is a legal document that allows you to appoint someone to make decisions on your behalf should you become unable to do so due to illness or incapacitation.

Consult a solicitor or estate planning professional for guidance on creating a comprehensive estate plan tailored to your needs and objectives.

In this chapter, we have explored the essential components of building a solid financial foundation, including emergency funds, insurance, and estate planning. By establishing a strong foundation, you will be better prepared to navigate the complexities of investing and achieve your financial goals. In the following chapters, we will delve deeper into budgeting, saving, and investing to help you build and grow your wealth.

Chapter 5: The Art of Budgeting

Mastering the art of budgeting is crucial to achieving financial success and building a strong foundation for your future. In this chapter, we will explore essential budgeting techniques, including the 50/30/20 rule, customising your budget, and tracking your expenses, to help you manage your finances effectively and reach your financial goals.

5.1 The 50/30/20 Rule

The 50/30/20 rule is a simple and widely-used budgeting guideline that can help you allocate your income to cover essential expenses, discretionary spending, and savings or debt repayment. According to this rule, you should allocate:

- 50% of your after-tax income to needs: This includes essential expenses such as housing, utilities, groceries, transportation, and healthcare.
- 30% of your after-tax income to wants: This includes discretionary spending on non-essential items or experiences, such as dining out, entertainment, and travel.
- 20% of your after-tax income to savings and debt repayment: This includes building an emergency fund, saving for future goals, investing, and paying off high-interest debt.

5.2 Customising Your Budget

While the 50/30/20 rule provides a helpful starting point, it's essential to customise your budget to suit your unique financial situation and goals. To create a personalised budget:

0.1. Assess your financial goals: Identify your short-term and long-term financial goals, such as building an emergency fund, paying off debt, or saving for a down payment on a home. Allocate a portion of your income to these goals within your budget.

0.2. Prioritise your expenses: Determine which expenses are most important to you and allocate your income accordingly. This may require cutting back on discretionary spending in certain areas to ensure you can cover essential expenses and work toward your financial goals.

0.3. Adjust your budget as needed: As your financial situation and priorities change, be prepared to adjust your budget accordingly. Regularly review your budget and make necessary adjustments to remain on track with your financial goals.

5.3 Tracking Your Expenses

Tracking your expenses is a crucial component of effective budgeting, as it enables you to monitor your spending habits and identify areas where you may be overspending. To track your expenses:

- Categorise your spending: Organise your expenses into categories, such as housing, utilities, groceries, transportation, and entertainment. This will help you see where your money is going and identify potential areas for savings.
- Use budgeting tools: Utilise budgeting apps or software to automatically track your spending and provide insights into your spending habits. Many budgeting tools also offer features to help you set spending limits and goals for each category.
- Review your expenses regularly: Regularly review your spending to ensure you are staying within your budget and making progress toward your financial goals. If you find that you are consistently overspending in certain areas, consider adjusting your budget or finding ways to cut back.

5.4 Budget Checklist

This table serves as a budget checklist to help you organise your monthly income and expenses. Feel free to modify the categories and subcategories to better suit your personal financial situation. Remember, creating a budget is a crucial step in taking control of your finances and working towards your financial goals.

Personal Tip: Make budgeting a habit by setting aside time each month to review your income and expenses. By consistently tracking your spending and identifying areas where you can cut back, you'll be better equipped to achieve your financial goals. For example, if you notice that you're overspending on dining out, consider setting a monthly limit.

In this chapter, we have explored the art of budgeting, including the 50/30/20 rule, customising your budget, and tracking your expenses. By implementing these techniques and remaining disciplined in your approach to budgeting, you can take control of your finances, make informed decisions about your spending habits, and work toward achieving your financial goals. In the following chapters, we will delve deeper into saving, investing, and managing your finances to help you build a secure financial future.

No.	Budget Category	Monthly Income/Expense	Notes
1	Income		
	- Salary		
	- Side Hustle		
	- Rental Income		
	- Investments		
	- Other		
2	Saving and investments		
	- Emergency Fund		
	- Retirement Savings		
	- Investments		
	- Other Savings Goals		
3	Housing		
	- Rent/mortgage		
	- Home Insurance		
	- Property Taxes		
	- Maintenance/ repairs		
	- Utilities		
4	Transportation		
	- Car Payment		
	- Car Transport		
	- Fuel		
	- Maintenance		
	- Public Transport		
5	Food		
	- Groceries		
	- Dining Out		
6	Insurance		
	- Health insurance		
	- Life Insurance		
	- Disability Insurance		

No.	Budget Category	Monthly Income/Expenses	Notes
7	Health and Wellness		
	- Gym Membership		
	- Medical Expenses		
	- Medications		
8	Debt Repayment		
	- Credit Card		
	- Student Loan		
	- Personal Loan		
9	Entertainment		
	- Streaming Services		
	- Hobbies		
	- Events		
10	Miscellaneous		
	- Clothing		
	- Gifts/Donations		
	- Travel		
	- Other		

Chapter 6: Saving and Investing Basics

Understanding the fundamentals of saving and investing is essential for building long-term wealth and financial security. In this chapter, we will cover the basics of savings accounts and Cash ISAs, the concepts of compound interest and time value of money, and the importance of diversification and asset allocation in building a robust investment portfolio.

6.1 Savings Accounts and Cash ISAs

Savings accounts and Cash ISAs (Individual Savings Accounts) are essential tools for building and maintaining an emergency fund, as well as saving for short-term financial goals.

- Savings accounts: These are interest-bearing accounts offered by banks and building societies, providing a safe and accessible place to store your money while earning a modest interest rate. Savings accounts are ideal for emergency funds and short-term goals, as they offer liquidity and low risk.
- Cash ISAs: A Cash ISA is a tax-efficient savings account available to UK residents. The interest earned on a Cash ISA is tax-free, making it an attractive option for savers looking to maximise their returns. Each tax year, you can contribute up to a specified limit, known as the ISA allowance.

6.2 Compound Interest and Time Value of Money

Two fundamental concepts in the world of saving and investing are compound interest and the time value of money.

0.1. Compound interest: This refers to the process by which interest is earned on both the initial principal amount and any interest that has previously been earned. Over time, compound interest can significantly increase the value of your savings or investments.

0.2. Time value of money: This concept asserts that a sum of money received today is worth more than the same sum received in the future, due to its potential earning capacity. The longer you invest or save, the more your money can grow, emphasising the importance of starting early and investing consistently.

To illustrate how compound interest works, let's consider a simple example. Assume you invest £1,000 in a savings account that offers a 5% annual interest rate, compounded annually. The table below demonstrates how the value of your investment will grow over time, thanks to compound interest.

Year	Starting Balance	Interest Earned	Ending Balance
1	£1,000	£50	£1,050
2	£1,050	£52.50	£1,102.50
3	£1,102.50	£55.63	£1,157.63
4	£1,157.63	£57.88	£1,215.51
5	£1,215.51	£60.78	£1,276.29

Over five years, the initial investment of £1,000 grows to £1,276.29, thanks to the power of compound interest. This demonstrates how compound interest can significantly increase the value of your savings or investments over time, especially when given enough time to grow.

Personal Tip: Embrace the power of compound interest by starting to save and invest early. Even small, regular contributions to your savings or investment accounts can grow significantly over time. For example, if you invest £100 per month with a 6% annual return, you would have over £100,000 after 30 years.

6.3 Diversification and Asset Allocation

Diversification and asset allocation are key strategies for managing risk and optimising returns in your investment portfolio.

- Diversification: This involves spreading your investments across various asset classes, industries, and geographic regions to reduce risk. A well-diversified portfolio can help protect your investments from market volatility and specific risks associated with individual assets.

- Asset allocation: This refers to the process of determining the optimal mix of asset classes in your portfolio, based on your financial goals, risk tolerance, and investment horizon. A balanced asset allocation helps to spread risk and maximise potential returns by investing in a variety of asset classes, each with different risk and return characteristics.

In this chapter, we have introduced the basics of saving and investing, including savings accounts and Cash ISAs, compound interest and time value of money, and diversification and asset allocation. By understanding these concepts and applying them to your financial planning, you can build a strong foundation for long-term wealth and financial security. In the following chapters, we will delve deeper into specific investment topics and strategies to help you further optimise your savings and investment portfolio.

Chapter 7: The UK Investment Landscape

Understanding the UK investment landscape is crucial for UK investors seeking to build a diverse and robust investment portfolio. In this chapter, we will explore various aspects of the UK investment environment, including taxation and regulation, stocks, bonds and funds, real estate and property investment, and alternative investments.

7.1 UK Taxation and Regulation

The UK investment landscape is governed by a set of tax laws and regulatory bodies designed to protect investors and maintain market integrity. Some key aspects of UK taxation and regulation include:

- Capital Gains Tax (CGT): This tax is levied on the profits made from selling assets, such as stocks, bonds, and property. Each tax year, individuals have a tax-free allowance for capital gains, after which they are taxed at their respective CGT rate.
- Dividend Tax: Dividends received from stocks are subject to dividend tax, with different tax rates depending on the individual's tax band.
- Individual Savings Accounts (ISAs) and pensions: These tax-advantaged accounts allow UK investors to save and invest without being subject to taxes on interest, dividends, or capital gains.

Financial Conduct Authority (FCA) and Prudential Regulation Authority (PRA): These regulatory bodies oversee the UK financial services industry, ensuring that financial firms operate in the best interest of consumers and maintain market stability.

7.2 Stocks, Bonds, and Funds

The UK investment landscape offers a wide range of investment options, such as stocks, bonds, and funds.

0.1. Stocks: Investors can buy shares in publicly traded UK companies listed on stock exchanges, such as the London Stock Exchange (LSE). Stocks offer the potential for capital appreciation and dividend income, albeit with higher risk compared to fixed-income investments.

0.2. Bonds: Bonds are fixed-income securities issued by governments or corporations. UK investors can invest in UK government bonds (gilts), corporate bonds, or other international bonds. Bonds typically provide regular interest payments and lower risk compared to stocks.

0.3. Funds: Investment funds, such as mutual funds, exchange-traded funds (ETFs), and index funds, offer a convenient way to invest in a diversified portfolio of stocks, bonds, or other assets. These funds can provide exposure to various sectors, industries, and geographical regions.

7.3 Real Estate and Property Investment

Real estate is a popular investment option in the UK, offering potential capital appreciation and rental income.

- Residential property: Investors can purchase residential properties to rent out or to sell for a profit. While property investment can offer attractive returns, it also requires significant upfront capital and ongoing management.
- Commercial property: Commercial properties, such as offices, retail spaces, and industrial properties, can offer diversification and higher rental yields than residential properties. However, commercial property investment may involve higher risks and capital requirements.
- Real Estate Investment Trusts (REITs): REITs allow investors to gain exposure to real estate without directly owning property. They are publicly traded companies that own and manage income-generating properties, offering investors the potential for capital appreciation and dividend income.

7.4 Alternative Investments

In addition to traditional investment options, UK investors can also explore alternative investments to diversify their portfolios and seek higher returns.

- Peer-to-peer lending: P2P lending platforms enable investors to lend money directly to individuals or businesses, offering the potential for higher interest rates than traditional savings accounts or bonds.

- Crowdfunding: Equity crowdfunding platforms allow investors to invest in early-stage companies in exchange for equity, offering the potential for significant capital appreciation if the companies succeed.
- Cryptocurrencies: Digital currencies, such as Bitcoin and Ethereum, have gained popularity as an alternative investment option. However, cryptocurrencies can be highly volatile and carry significant risks.

In addition to the regulated investments discussed in this chapter, there are also non-regulated investments that UK investors may come across. Non-regulated investments refer to investment products or schemes that fall outside the jurisdiction of the UK's regulatory bodies, such as the Financial Conduct Authority (FCA) and the Prudential Regulation Authority (PRA).

7.5 Non-Regulated Investment Warning

Some examples of non-regulated investments include:

- Unlisted shares: Shares of private companies that are not listed on a public stock exchange are considered non-regulated investments. Investing in unlisted shares can offer the potential for high returns, but also involves higher risk and reduced liquidity compared to listed shares.
- Land banking schemes: These schemes involve purchasing undeveloped land with the hope that its value will increase due to future development or planning permission changes. While land banking can offer potential for capital appreciation, it is an unregulated investment and carries significant risks, including the possibility of fraud or mismanagement.
- Wine, art, and collectables: Investing in fine wine, art, or collectable items, such as coins or stamps, can offer diversification and potential for capital appreciation. However, these investments are unregulated and can be subject to high transaction costs, illiquidity, and market volatility.

When considering non-regulated investments, it's important to exercise caution and conduct thorough due diligence. These investments often carry higher risks and may not be covered by the

Financial Services Compensation Scheme (FSCS), which protects consumers when authorised financial firms fail.

Before investing in non-regulated products or schemes, make sure to research the investment thoroughly, understand the associated risks, and seek professional advice if needed. It's essential to ensure that the investment aligns with your financial goals, risk tolerance, and investment horizon, and that you are comfortable with the potential risks involved.

In this chapter, we have provided an overview of the UK investment landscape, including key aspects of taxation and regulation, as well as various investment options such as stocks, bonds, funds, real estate, and alternative investments. By understanding the opportunities and challenges associated with each investment type, UK investors can make informed decisions about how to allocate their assets and build a diverse and robust investment portfolio tailored to their financial goals and risk tolerance.

As you navigate the UK investment landscape, remember to continuously monitor your investments and adjust your portfolio as needed to stay on track with your financial goals. Regularly reviewing and rebalancing your portfolio can help ensure that your asset allocation remains aligned with your risk tolerance and investment objectives, allowing you to optimise your returns and manage risk effectively.

In the chapters that follow, we will delve deeper into various investment strategies and financial planning techniques, equipping you with the knowledge and tools necessary to make the most of your investments and achieve long-term financial success.

Chapter 8: Retirement Planning in the UK

Retirement planning is an essential aspect of long-term financial planning, ensuring that you have sufficient funds to maintain a comfortable lifestyle in your later years. In this chapter, we will discuss various aspects of retirement planning in the UK, including state and workplace pensions, personal pensions and SIPPs, Lifetime ISAs, and retirement strategies. We will also provide some relevant statistics and sources to help you make informed decisions about your retirement planning.

8.1 State Pension and Workplace Pensions

State and workplace pensions form the foundation of retirement planning for most UK residents.

- State Pension: The UK State Pension is a government-backed pension scheme that provides a regular income to eligible retirees based on their National Insurance contributions. The full new State Pension is £203.85 per week as of 2023/2024, but the actual amount you receive will depend on your National Insurance record (source: GOV.UK). Please also note, this is subject to change depending on government.
- Workplace Pensions: Since the introduction of automatic enrolment, most UK employees are enrolled in a workplace pension scheme, with both employees and employers contributing a percentage of the employee's salary towards the pension fund. The minimum auto-enrolment contributions are 8% of qualifying earnings, with at least 3% coming from the employer (source: The Pensions Regulator).

8.2 Personal Pensions and SIPPs

In addition to state and workplace pensions, personal pensions and Self-Invested Personal Pensions (SIPPs) provide further opportunities to save for retirement.

- Personal Pensions: These are private pension schemes offered by insurance companies, banks, and other financial institutions. Personal pensions allow individuals to make regular or lump-sum contributions and invest the funds in a range of investment options. The pension provider claims tax relief on your contributions and adds it to your pension pot.

- SIPPs: A SIPP is a type of personal pension that offers more flexibility and control over investment choices, allowing individuals to invest in a wider range of assets, including stocks, bonds, and commercial property.

Personal Tip: Don't underestimate the importance of planning for retirement. Start saving early, and review your pension arrangements regularly to ensure that you're on track to achieve your desired retirement lifestyle. For example, if you're not contributing enough to your workplace pension, consider increasing your contributions or setting up a personal pension.

Pros and Cons of Lifestyling Funds within Pensions

Lifestyling funds, also known as target-date funds or lifestyle funds, are a type of pension investment option designed to automatically adjust the allocation of assets within your pension portfolio as you approach retirement. These funds aim to strike a balance between growth and risk management by gradually shifting from higher-risk investments, such as equities, to lower-risk investments, such as bonds and cash, as you near retirement. In this insert, we will explore the pros and cons of lifestyling funds within pensions.

Pros of Lifestyling Funds:

- Simplicity: Lifestyling funds offer a hands-off approach to retirement planning, as they automatically adjust your asset allocation based on your age and target retirement date. This can be particularly beneficial for individuals who may lack the time or expertise to actively manage their pension investments.

- Risk management: By gradually shifting the investment mix from higher-risk assets to lower-risk assets as you approach retirement, lifestyling funds aim to reduce the potential impact of market volatility on your pension pot. This can help protect your retirement savings from significant market downturns in the years leading up to retirement.

- Diversification: Lifestyling funds typically invest in a diverse range of assets, such as equities, bonds, and cash, which can help spread risk and potentially improve long-term returns.

Cons of Lifestyling Funds:

- One-size-fits-all approach: Lifestyling funds use a standardised approach to asset allocation based on age and target retirement date, which may not be suitable for everyone. Individual investors may have unique circumstances, risk tolerances, or financial goals that are not adequately addressed by a lifestyling fund.
- Limited flexibility: With lifestyling funds, investors have limited control over their investment choices, as the fund manager determines the asset allocation and adjusts it over time. This lack of flexibility can be a drawback for investors who wish to take a more active role in managing their pension investments.
- Potential for lower returns: Lifestyling funds typically prioritise risk management over maximising returns, particularly as the investor approaches retirement. As a result, these funds may generate lower returns compared to more aggressive investment strategies, potentially impacting your overall retirement savings.

In summary, lifestyling funds within pensions can offer a simple, risk-managed approach to retirement planning, but they may not be suitable for all investors. It's important to carefully consider the pros and cons of lifestyling funds and assess whether this investment option aligns with your individual financial goals, risk tolerance, and investment preferences.

8.3 Lifetime ISAs

Lifetime ISAs (LISAs) are a tax-efficient savings vehicle designed to help UK residents save for their first home or retirement.

Individuals aged 18-39 can open a LISA and contribute up to £4,000 per tax year. The government adds a 25% bonus on contributions, up to £1,000 per year (source: GOV.UK).

Funds in a LISA can be withdrawn tax-free after age 60 or to purchase a first home worth up to £450,000. Withdrawals for other purposes are subject to a penalty.

8.4 Retirement Strategies

Effective retirement planning requires a tailored approach based on your individual financial goals, risk tolerance, and investment horizon. Some strategies to consider include:

0.1. Assessing your retirement income needs and setting savings goals accordingly

0.2. Diversifying your investments to spread risk and optimise returns

0.3. Regularly reviewing and adjusting your pension contributions and investment mix

0.4. Considering additional sources of retirement income, such as property investments or part-time work

8.5 Flexible Drawdown

Flexible drawdown is a feature of pension arrangements in the UK, allowing retirees to access their pension funds in a more flexible manner. This option provides greater control over how and when you withdraw funds from your pension, giving you the opportunity to tailor your retirement income to your specific needs and circumstances. In this insert, we will explain how flexible drawdown works and discuss the associated risks.

How Flexible Drawdown Works:

- Accessing funds: With flexible drawdown, you can withdraw any amount from your pension at any time, subject to your pension provider's terms and conditions. You can choose to take lump sums or regular income payments, depending on your financial needs and preferences.
- Tax implications: The first 25% of your pension pot can typically be withdrawn tax-free. However, any withdrawals beyond this amount will be subject to income tax at your marginal rate.
- Investment growth: Unlike purchasing an annuity, where your pension pot is exchanged for a guaranteed income for life, your pension funds remain invested with flexible

drawdown. This means that your investments have the potential to grow over time, potentially increasing your retirement income.

- Pension provider requirements: Flexible drawdown is not automatically available with every pension scheme. You may need to transfer your pension to a provider that offers this option, and fees may apply for the transfer and ongoing management of your pension.

Risks of Flexible Drawdown:

- Running out of money: One of the main risks associated with flexible drawdown is the possibility of depleting your pension funds prematurely, particularly if you withdraw large sums or if your investments perform poorly. It's crucial to manage your withdrawals carefully and consider the impact of market fluctuations on your pension pot.
- Investment risk: As your pension funds remain invested, you are exposed to market risks and volatility, which could potentially reduce the value of your pension pot over time.
- Tax implications: Poorly managed withdrawals could result in higher income tax liability. It's essential to plan your withdrawals strategically to minimise your tax burden.
- Inflation risk: If your pension funds are not growing at a rate that keeps pace with inflation, your purchasing power may erode over time, reducing the value of your retirement income.

Flexible drawdown offers greater control and flexibility in managing your retirement income, but it also comes with increased risks and responsibilities. It's essential to carefully consider your financial needs, risk tolerance, and investment strategy when deciding whether flexible drawdown is the right option for you. Consulting with a financial advisor can provide valuable guidance in making this important decision.

8.6 Sequence of Returns Risk in Drawdown

Sequence of returns risk refers to the potential impact of the order in which investment returns occur on the sustainability of a retirement portfolio during the drawdown phase. This risk is particularly relevant for retirees who rely on their investments to provide a steady income.

The sequence of returns risk can significantly affect the longevity of a retirement portfolio, especially during the early years of retirement. If a retiree experiences a series of negative returns early in retirement, the value of their portfolio may decline rapidly, reducing its ability to recover and potentially leading to the depletion of retirement assets sooner than anticipated.

Consider the following table illustrating the impact of sequence of returns risk on a retirement portfolio with an initial value of £1,000,000 and an annual withdrawal of £40,000:

Year	Scenario 1: Good Returns Early	Scenario 2: Poor Returns Early
1	£1,040,000 (+4%)	£920,000 (-8%)
2	£1,081,600 (+4%)	£841,600 (-8%)
3	£1,124,864 (+4%)	£767,344 (-8%)
4	£1,169,898 (+4%)	£697,037 (-8%)
5	£1,216,814 (+4%)	£630,681 (-8%)

In Scenario 1, the portfolio experiences positive returns early in retirement, while in Scenario 2, the portfolio suffers poor returns early on. By the end of the fifth year, the portfolio value in Scenario 1 is significantly higher than in Scenario 2, despite both scenarios having the same average return.

A study by Finke, Pfau, and Blanchett (2013) found that the sequence of returns risk can increase the likelihood of portfolio depletion during retirement by as much as 18% for a retiree with a 4% withdrawal rate (source: Finke, Pfau, and Blanchett, 2013).

To manage the sequence of returns risk, retirees can consider the following strategies:

- Adjusting withdrawal rates: Reducing withdrawal rates during periods of poor investment performance can help preserve the portfolio's value and improve its sustainability.
- Maintaining a cash reserve: Having a cash reserve to cover living expenses during market downturns can help avoid selling investments at a loss.
- Diversifying investments: A diversified portfolio can help

reduce the impact of poor returns in any single asset class.

By understanding the sequence of returns risk and implementing strategies to address it, retirees can help ensure the sustainability of their retirement portfolios and maintain their desired lifestyle throughout retirement.

In conclusion, retirement planning in the UK involves a combination of state and workplace pensions, personal pensions and SIPPs, and tax-efficient savings vehicles such as Lifetime ISAs. By understanding the various aspects of retirement planning and implementing tailored strategies, you can work towards building a secure and comfortable retirement. In the following chapters, we will discuss additional financial planning topics and strategies to help you achieve your long-term financial goals and create a comprehensive financial plan.

8.7 Defined Benefit Pensions vs. Money Purchase Pensions

Understanding the differences between defined benefit pensions and money purchase pensions is crucial when planning for your retirement. These two types of pension schemes have distinct features, benefits, and risks, which can significantly impact your retirement income.

Defined Benefit Pensions:

Defined benefit pensions, also known as final salary pensions, provide a guaranteed income for life when you retire. The amount you receive is based on a formula that takes into account your salary, years of service, and a specific accrual rate. Your employer is responsible for funding the pension and ensuring that there's enough money to pay your benefits. As a result, the investment risk lies with the employer, not the employee.

Key features:

- Guaranteed income for life
- Income based on salary, years of service, and accrual rate
- Employer takes on the investment risk

Money Purchase Pensions:

Money purchase pensions, also known as defined contribution pensions, are retirement schemes where you and your employer contribute a percentage of your salary to a pension fund. The money in the fund is then invested in assets like stocks, bonds, and property. The final amount you receive at retirement depends on the total contributions made and the investment performance of the fund. In this case, the investment risk is borne by the employee, not the employer.

Key features:

- Retirement income depends on contributions and investment performance
- No guaranteed income
- Employee takes on the investment risk

	Defined Benefits Pensions	Money Purchase Pensions
Type of Income	Guaranteed	Variable
Income Calculation	Based on salary, years of service, and accrual rate	Based on contributions and investment performance
Investment Risk	Employer	employee
Employers Responsibility	Funding the pension and managing the investment risk	Contributing a percentage of the employee's salary

Understanding the key differences between defined benefit and money purchase pensions can help you make more informed decisions about your retirement planning. Be sure to consider the features, benefits, and risks associated with each type of pension scheme when evaluating your options and planning for your financial future.

Personal Tip: Transferring a defined benefit pension scheme comes with significant risks and should be approached with caution. Defined benefit pensions provide a guaranteed income for life, which can be difficult to replicate with other types of pension schemes. If you're considering transferring your defined benefit pension, it's essential to seek advice from a specialist pension transfer adviser who can help you understand the potential risks, benefits, and long-term implications of making such a decision. Remember that transferring a defined benefit pension is not suitable for everyone and should only be done after thorough analysis and consultation with a qualified professional.

Chapter 9: Tax-Efficient Investing

Tax-efficient investing is a key component of successful financial planning, as it enables you to maximise your returns and minimise the impact of taxes on your investments. In this chapter, we will discuss various tax-efficient investment options available in the UK, including Individual Savings Accounts (ISAs), Venture Capital Trusts (VCTs), Enterprise Investment Schemes (EIS), and Seed Enterprise Investment Schemes (SEIS). It's important to note that these investment options carry various risks, and it's essential to consider these risks in the context of your overall investment strategy and financial goals.

9.1 Understanding ISAs (Individual Savings Accounts)

ISAs are tax-advantaged savings and investment accounts designed to encourage UK residents to save and invest. They offer a range of benefits, including:

- No tax on interest, dividends, or capital gains
- A wide variety of investment options, such as cash, stocks, and bonds
- An annual ISA allowance, which is £20,000 for the 2021/2022 tax year (source: GOV.UK)

There are several types of ISAs available, including Cash ISAs, Stocks and Shares ISAs, Innovative Finance ISAs, and Lifetime ISAs, each with its own features and eligibility criteria. While ISAs offer significant tax benefits, it's important to note that the value of investments can go up or down, and you may get back less than you originally invested.

Personal Tip: Make the most of tax-advantaged accounts like ISAs, pensions, and VCTs to minimise your tax liabilities and maximise your investment returns. For example, consider using your annual ISA allowance to invest in a stocks and shares ISA, which allows your investments to grow tax-free.

9.2 Venture Capital Trusts (VCTs)

VCTs are publicly-listed investment companies that invest in small, high-growth businesses. They offer a range of tax benefits to UK investors, including:

- 30% income tax relief on investments up to £200,000 per tax year, provided the shares are held for at least five years (source: GOV.UK)
- Tax-free dividends
- No capital gains tax on the sale of VCT shares

However, VCTs also carry significant risks, as they invest in smaller, unlisted companies, which are typically more volatile and less liquid than larger, listed companies. It's important to carefully consider the risks associated with VCT investments and ensure they align with your risk tolerance and investment objectives.

9.3 Enterprise Investment Schemes (EIS)

EIS is a government-backed scheme designed to encourage investment in small, high-risk companies. It offers various tax benefits to UK investors, including:

- 30% income tax relief on investments up to £1 million per tax year, or £2 million if at least £1 million is invested in knowledge-intensive companies (source: GOV.UK)
- Capital gains tax deferral on gains reinvested in EIS-eligible companies
- No capital gains tax on the sale of EIS shares held for at least three years
- Loss relief, allowing investors to offset losses against their income tax liability

EIS investments carry significant risks due to the nature of the companies being invested in. The value of these investments can fluctuate, and there is a risk of losing your entire investment. As with VCTs, it's essential to weigh the risks and potential rewards before investing in EIS-eligible companies.

9.4 Seed Enterprise Investment Schemes (SEIS)

SEIS is an initiative similar to EIS, but it focuses on investing in early-stage, high-risk start-ups. The scheme offers even more substantial tax benefits to UK investors, including:

- 50% income tax relief on investments up to £100,000 per tax year (source: GOV.UK)
- No capital gains tax on the sale of SEIS shares held for at least three years
- Capital gains tax reinvestment relief, allowing investors to defer capital gains tax on gains reinvested in SEIS-eligible companies
- Loss relief, enabling investors to offset losses against their income tax liability

However, SEIS investments carry a higher level of risk compared to other tax-efficient investment options, as they involve investing in early-stage start-ups with limited operating history and uncertain growth prospects. The potential for significant losses is more considerable, and there is a risk of losing your entire investment. As with EIS and VCTs, it's crucial to carefully consider the risks associated with SEIS investments and ensure they align with your risk tolerance and investment objectives.

In conclusion, tax-efficient investing is a critical aspect of maximising your investment returns and minimising your tax liabilities. Understanding the various tax-efficient investment options available in the UK, such as ISAs, VCTs, EIS, and SEIS, can help you make informed decisions about which options best suit your financial goals, risk tolerance, and investment preferences. However, it's essential to be aware of the risks associated with these investments, particularly with VCTs, EIS, and SEIS, which involve investing in smaller, high-risk companies. Always consider seeking professional advice before making any investment decisions.

Chapter 10: Building Your Investment Portfolio

Constructing an investment portfolio is an essential aspect of achieving your financial goals. The right portfolio should reflect your risk tolerance, investment horizon, and financial objectives. In this chapter, we will discuss various approaches to building your investment portfolio, including DIY vs. professional advice, robo-advisors and platforms, and the importance of portfolio rebalancing and monitoring. We will also provide relevant statistics and sources to help you make informed decisions about your investment strategy.

10.1 DIY vs. Professional Advice

Investors have two primary options when building their investment portfolios: doing it themselves (DIY) or seeking professional advice.

0.1. DIY: Many investors opt to manage their portfolios independently, selecting their investments and making decisions without the guidance of a financial advisor. This approach can be cost-effective, as it avoids advisory fees, but requires a good understanding of financial markets and investment principles. According to a 2020 survey by Finder UK, 41% of UK adults manage their investments independently (source: Finder UK).

0.2. Professional Advice: Alternatively, investors can work with a financial advisor who will provide tailored investment advice and portfolio management services based on their financial goals and risk tolerance. This approach can offer peace of mind and expert guidance but comes with additional fees. In the same survey, 24% of UK adults used a financial advisor to manage their investments (source: Finder UK).

When considering whether to manage your investments independently (DIY) or seek professional advice, it's essential to understand the potential risks and benefits associated with each approach. In this section, we will expand on the risks of DIY investing compared to seeking professional advice and provide relevant statistics and sources to support these points.

DIY Investing Risks:

- Lack of expertise: Many individual investors may lack the knowledge and experience necessary to make informed investment decisions. This can lead to under-performance or significant losses in their portfolios. According to a 2017 study by the Financial Conduct Authority (FCA), DIY investors were more likely to exhibit biases and make investment decisions based on misconceptions compared to investors who sought professional advice (source: FCA).
- Emotional decision-making: DIY investors may be more prone to making emotional decisions, leading to impulsive buying or selling during market fluctuations. This can result in reduced returns and increased risk. A study by Dalbar found that the average DIY investor under-performed the market by 1.7% per year over 20 years, primarily due to poor market timing and emotional decision-making (source: Dalbar).
- Limited diversification and asset allocation: DIY investors may struggle with diversification and asset allocation, leading to a less balanced and riskier portfolio. A study by Vanguard found that professional financial advisors can add up to 3% in net portfolio returns through proper asset allocation and portfolio construction (source: Vanguard).

Professional Advice Benefits:

- Expert guidance: Financial advisors have the expertise and experience to help investors make informed decisions, construct well-diversified portfolios, and navigate complex financial markets. A study by the International Longevity Centre UK found that individuals who received financial advice accumulated 17% more in financial assets and 16% more in pension wealth than their non-advised counterparts (source: ILC-UK).
- Personalised strategy: Professional advisors can create tailored investment strategies based on an individual's financial goals, risk tolerance, and investment horizon. This personalised approach can help investors stay on track towards their financial objectives.
- Ongoing support and monitoring: Financial advisors provide ongoing support, monitoring, and adjustments to an

investor's portfolio as market conditions and personal circumstances change. This can help ensure that the portfolio remains aligned with the investor's goals and risk tolerance over time.

In conclusion, while DIY investing can be cost-effective and offer a sense of control over one's investments, it comes with several risks, including a lack of expertise, emotional decision-making, and limited diversification. On the other hand, seeking professional advice can provide expert guidance, personalised strategies, and ongoing support, which can help investors achieve better long-term results. It's crucial to weigh these risks and benefits when deciding between DIY investing and seeking professional advice, considering your financial goals, risk tolerance, and investment preferences.

10.2 Robo-Advisors and Platforms

Another option for building an investment portfolio is using robo-advisors and investment platforms. These services leverage technology and algorithms to create and manage investment portfolios based on your financial goals and risk tolerance.

- Robo-Advisors: Robo-advisors offer automated, algorithm-driven investment management services, typically at a lower cost than traditional financial advisors. Some popular robo-advisors in the UK include Nutmeg, Wealthify, and Moneyfarm.
- Platforms: Investment platforms allow investors to manage and monitor their portfolios through a single online interface. These platforms often provide access to a wide range of investment options, including stocks, bonds, funds, and more. Popular platforms in the UK include Hargreaves Lansdown, AJ Bell Youinvest, and Interactive Investor.

10.3 Portfolio Rebalancing and Monitoring

Once you've built your investment portfolio, it's essential to regularly monitor and rebalance it to maintain the desired level of risk and return. Portfolio rebalancing involves adjusting your asset allocation to bring it back in line with your original investment strategy.

- Rebalancing can help manage risk by ensuring your portfolio doesn't become overly concentrated in a particular asset class due to market fluctuations.
- Regular monitoring allows you to assess your portfolio's performance, identify under-performing investments, and make adjustments as needed to stay on track towards your financial goals.

Rebalancing GIA Portfolios and Capital Gains Tax Considerations

When rebalancing a General Investment Account (GIA) portfolio, it's important to be mindful of the potential tax implications, particularly regarding Capital Gains Tax (CGT). Capital Gains Tax is a tax on the profit when you sell or dispose of an asset that has increased in value. In the context of investment portfolios, this typically applies to the sale of shares, bonds, or other investments that have appreciated in value.

Rebalancing your GIA portfolio might involve selling certain assets that have performed well, potentially triggering a capital gains tax liability. As of the 2023/2024 tax year, the CGT allowance is £6,000 per individual, meaning you can realise gains up to this amount without incurring any tax (source: GOV.UK). Gains exceeding the allowance are subject to CGT at rates of 10% or 20% for basic rate taxpayers and 20% or 28% for higher or additional rate taxpayers, depending on the asset type.

To manage your CGT liability when rebalancing your GIA portfolio, consider the following strategies:

0.1. Utilise your annual CGT allowance: Be aware of your annual CGT allowance and try to keep your realised gains within this limit when rebalancing your portfolio. You can also consider spreading your rebalancing activities over multiple tax years to make the most of your annual allowance.

0.2. Offset gains with losses: If you have realised losses from the sale of other investments, you can offset these against your realised gains to reduce your overall CGT liability. Keep track of your capital losses and gains to ensure you are optimising your tax position.

0.3. Use tax-efficient wrappers: Consider using tax-efficient investment vehicles, such as ISAs or pensions, to hold your investments. These wrappers protect your investments from CGT and can help you manage your overall tax liability when rebalancing your portfolio.

In summary, when rebalancing your GIA portfolio, it's essential to be aware of the potential tax implications, particularly regarding Capital Gains Tax. By carefully managing your CGT liability and utilising tax-efficient strategies, you can minimise the impact of taxes on your investment returns and maintain a well-balanced portfolio aligned with your financial goals.

Personal Tip: Stay disciplined and focused on your long-term goals, rather than reacting to short-term market fluctuations. Regularly review and rebalance your portfolio to ensure that it remains aligned with your objectives and risk tolerance. For example, if your portfolio has become overweight in equities due to strong market performance, consider rebalancing by selling some equities and reinvesting the proceeds in bonds or other asset classes.

10.4 Active vs. Passive Funds - Understanding Unit Trusts and OEICs

Investing in funds can be an effective way to diversify your portfolio and gain exposure to various asset classes. Before diving into the world of funds, it's important to understand the differences between active and passive funds and the types of fund structures, such as unit trusts and OEICs (Open-Ended Investment Companies).

What is a Fund?

A fund is a pooled investment vehicle that collects money from multiple investors and uses that capital to buy a diversified portfolio of assets, such as stocks, bonds, or property. The two most common types of funds in the UK are unit trusts and OEICs.

- Unit Trusts: A unit trust is an open-ended fund that issues units to investors. The price of these units fluctuates based on the value of the underlying assets. Unit trusts are managed by a fund manager who makes investment decisions on behalf of the investors.

- OEICs: An OEIC operates similarly to a unit trust but has a more flexible structure. It is structured as a company and issues shares instead of units. Like unit trusts, OEICs are managed by a fund manager who makes investment decisions for the fund.

Active Funds vs. Passive Funds

- Active Funds: In an actively managed fund, the fund manager selects and manages the fund's investments, aiming to outperform a specific benchmark or index. Active funds typically have higher fees due to the research and expertise required to make investment decisions.
- Passive Funds: A passive fund, also known as an index fund or tracker fund, aims to replicate the performance of a specific benchmark or index, such as the FTSE 100 or S&P 500. Passive funds have lower fees compared to active funds, as they do not require active management and decision-making by a fund manager.

Selecting a Fund for Your Goals, Objectives, and Risk Profile

When selecting a fund for your investment portfolio, consider the following factors:

- Investment Objectives: Define your investment goals, such as capital growth, income generation, or capital preservation. Choose a fund that aligns with your objectives and has a track record of meeting them.
- Risk Tolerance: Evaluate your risk tolerance and select a fund with a risk profile that matches your comfort level. Passive funds may be more suitable for risk-averse investors, while active funds might be more appropriate for those willing to take on more risk for potentially higher returns.
- Costs and Fees: Compare the fees and charges associated with different funds, as they can impact your investment returns. Passive funds typically have lower fees than active funds, but it's essential to weigh the potential benefits of active management against the higher costs.

- Fund Manager's Track Record: Research the fund manager's performance history and expertise in managing similar funds or asset classes. This can provide insight into their ability to navigate various market conditions and deliver consistent results.

By understanding the differences between active and passive funds and considering your investment goals, risk tolerance, and other factors, you can make more informed decisions when selecting a fund that aligns with your financial objectives.

In conclusion, building an investment portfolio is a critical aspect of achieving your financial goals, and there are various approaches to consider, including DIY, professional advice, robo-advisors, and investment platforms. It's essential to regularly monitor and rebalance your portfolio to maintain the desired risk and return levels. By understanding the different approaches to building your investment portfolio and considering your risk tolerance, investment horizon, and financial objectives, you can make informed decisions that will set you on the path towards long-term financial success.

Chapter 11: Sustainable and Socially Responsible Investing

As environmental, social, and governance (ESG) issues continue to gain prominence, an increasing number of investors are looking for sustainable and socially responsible investment opportunities. In this chapter, we will discuss key concepts related to sustainable and socially responsible investing, including ESG criteria, green and social bonds, and impact investing. We will also provide relevant statistics and sources to help you make informed decisions about incorporating sustainable investing into your portfolio.

11.1 Understanding ESG Criteria

ESG criteria refer to a set of non-financial factors that investors can use to evaluate a company's performance, sustainability, and ethical practices. ESG criteria typically fall into three categories:

- Environmental: Factors related to a company's impact on the environment, including energy use, pollution, waste management, and natural resource conservation.
- Social: Factors related to a company's relationships with its employees, customers, and communities, including labour practices, diversity and inclusion, and human rights.
- Governance: Factors related to a company's corporate governance practices, including board diversity, executive compensation, and shareholder rights.

According to a 2020 survey by the UK Sustainable Investment and Finance Association (UKSIF), 42% of UK investors consider ESG factors when making investment decisions (source: UKSIF).

Personal Tip: Align your investments with your personal values by considering ESG criteria when selecting investment options. Research companies and funds that prioritise environmental, social, and governance factors, and be aware of the potential for greenwashing. For example, consider investing in a fund that specifically targets companies with strong environmental practices or a positive impact on society.

11.2 Green and Social Bonds

Green and social bonds are fixed-income securities issued by governments, corporations, and financial institutions to finance projects with positive environmental and social outcomes.

- Green Bonds: Green bonds are used to finance projects that contribute to environmental sustainability, such as renewable energy, energy efficiency, and pollution reduction initiatives. The global green bond market reached $1 trillion in cumulative issuance in 2020 (source: Climate Bonds Initiative).
- Social Bonds: Social bonds are used to finance projects that address social challenges, such as affordable housing, education, and healthcare. The global social bond market experienced significant growth in 2020, with issuance reaching $162.7 billion, up from $18.9 billion in 2019 (source: Environmental Finance).

11.3 Impact Investing

Impact investing refers to investments made with the intention of generating a measurable, positive social or environmental impact alongside a financial return. Impact investments can be made across various asset classes, including stocks, bonds, and private equity.

According to the Global Impact Investing Network (GIIN), the global impact investing market was valued at $715 billion in 2020, representing a 42.4% increase from 2019 (source: GIIN).

11.4 Green Washing

As sustainable and socially responsible investing gains popularity, it's crucial to be aware of the potential for "greenwashing." Greenwashing refers to the practice of companies or investment products misleading consumers by presenting themselves as more environmentally friendly or socially responsible than they genuinely are.

Greenwashing can take various forms, such as overstating the environmental benefits of a product or service, making vague or unsubstantiated claims about a company's sustainability practices, or using misleading marketing materials to create a false impression of environmental commitment.

To avoid falling victim to greenwashing, consider the following tips when evaluating sustainable investment options:

0.1. Research the investment: Carefully review the investment's prospectus or marketing materials to understand how it incorporates ESG factors or supports sustainable initiatives. Be wary of vague or unsubstantiated claims and look for concrete examples of the investment's impact.

0.2. Verify third-party certifications: Some sustainable investments may have third-party certifications or ratings, such as those from the Global Reporting Initiative (GRI), the Carbon Disclosure Project (CDP), or MSCI ESG Ratings. These certifications can provide an additional layer of assurance regarding the investment's commitment to sustainability. However, it's essential to understand the criteria and methodology behind these certifications to assess their credibility.

0.3. Monitor performance: Once you've invested in a sustainable investment product, continue to monitor its performance and impact. Regularly review the company's annual sustainability reports or updates from the investment manager to ensure that the investment continues to align with your sustainability goals and expectations.

By being vigilant and conducting thorough research, you can avoid greenwashing and ensure that your sustainable investments genuinely contribute to positive environmental and social outcomes.

In conclusion, sustainable and socially responsible investing offers investors the opportunity to align their financial goals with their values, supporting positive environmental and social outcomes. By understanding ESG criteria, green and social bonds, and impact investing, you can make informed decisions about incorporating sustainable investments into your portfolio, contributing to a more sustainable and equitable future.

Chapter 12: Navigating Economic Cycles and Market Volatility

Economic cycles and market volatility can significantly impact investment performance. In this chapter, we will discuss key aspects of navigating these fluctuations, including the role of central banks, the impact of Brexit and global events, coping with market fluctuations, and the risks associated with attempting to time markets.

12.1 The Role of Central Banks

Central banks play a crucial role in managing a country's economy and financial system. Their primary functions include setting interest rates, managing inflation, and ensuring the stability of the financial system. By understanding the actions and policies of central banks, such as the Bank of England, investors can gain insights into potential economic trends and market movements.

12.2 The Impact of Brexit and Global Events

Brexit and other global events can have significant effects on financial markets and investment performance. For example, Brexit has led to increased uncertainty and volatility in the UK and European financial markets. By staying informed about these events and their potential implications, investors can make more informed decisions about their investment strategies and risk exposure.

12.3 Coping with Market Fluctuations

Market fluctuations are a natural part of the investment process, and investors should be prepared to navigate these ups and downs. Some strategies to cope with market fluctuations include:

- Maintaining a diversified portfolio: By diversifying your investments across different asset classes and sectors, you can help reduce the impact of market volatility on your portfolio.
- Focusing on long-term goals: Avoid making impulsive decisions during market fluctuations and stay focused on your long-term investment objectives.

- Pound-cost averaging: Regularly investing a fixed amount over time, regardless of market conditions, can help you avoid trying to time the market and reduce the impact of market fluctuations on your investments.

12.4 The Risks of Trying to Time Markets

Attempting to time the market by predicting when to buy or sell investments can be a risky strategy. Market timing is difficult to execute successfully, even for professional investors, and can lead to reduced investment returns and increased risk. A study by Fidelity Investments found that investors who stayed fully invested in the stock market between 1980 and 2018 experienced an average annual return of 8.15%, while those who missed the best 30 days during that period saw their returns drop to 4.45% (source: Fidelity Investments).

In conclusion, navigating economic cycles and market volatility is an essential aspect of successful investing. By understanding the role of central banks, staying informed about global events, adopting strategies to cope with market fluctuations, and avoiding the risks of trying to time markets, investors can better manage their investments and achieve their financial goals.

Personal Tip: Stay informed about the broader economic environment and how it may impact your investments, but avoid making impulsive decisions based on short-term events. Focus on your long-term goals and maintain a well-diversified portfolio to help manage market fluctuations. For example, during times of economic uncertainty, resist the urge to sell out of fear and instead, remind yourself of your long-term objectives..

Chapter 13: Protecting Your Wealth

Preserving and protecting your wealth is a crucial aspect of long-term financial planning. In this chapter, we will discuss key strategies for safeguarding your wealth, including addressing inflation and currency risks, tax planning and mitigation, and estate preservation strategies. We will also provide relevant statistics and sources to support these points.

13.1 Inflation and Currency Risks

Inflation refers to the rate at which the general price level of goods and services in an economy increases over time, eroding the purchasing power of money. Currency risk, on the other hand, arises from fluctuations in exchange rates when holding investments in foreign currencies. Both inflation and currency risks can impact the real value of your investments.

To illustrate the effect of inflation, consider the table below, which shows the erosion of £100,000 in purchasing power over different periods at a 2% annual inflation rate:

Years	Future Value
5	£90,391
10	£81,707
15	£74,067
20	£67,296

(Source: Bank of England Inflation Calculator)

Some strategies to protect your wealth from inflation and currency risks include:

0.1. Investing in inflation-linked assets: Assets such as inflation-linked bonds or real estate can help preserve your wealth during periods of rising inflation.

0.2. Diversifying your portfolio: Including investments in different currencies and regions can help mitigate currency risks.

0.3. Hedging currency exposure: Using financial instruments such as currency forwards or options can help manage currency risks in your investment portfolio.

13.2 Tax Planning and Mitigation

Effective tax planning and mitigation can help you preserve more of your wealth for yourself and future generations. Strategies to consider include:

- Utilising tax-efficient investment vehicles: ISAs, pensions, and other tax-advantaged accounts can help minimise your tax liabilities on investment income and capital gains.
- Maximising personal allowances and reliefs: Ensuring you utilise your personal tax allowances and reliefs, such as the annual capital gains tax allowance, can help reduce your overall tax burden.
- Seeking professional advice: A tax professional can help you identify and implement tax planning strategies tailored to your individual circumstances.

13.3 Estate Preservation Strategies

Estate preservation strategies aim to protect your wealth for your beneficiaries and minimise the impact of inheritance tax (IHT). Some strategies to consider include:

- Gifting assets: Making gifts to family members or setting up trusts can help reduce the value of your estate subject to IHT, provided certain conditions are met.
- Life insurance policies: Taking out a life insurance policy written in trust can help provide a lump sum to cover potential IHT liabilities for your beneficiaries.
- Business property relief (BPR): Investing in BPR-qualifying assets, such as shares in certain unlisted companies, can provide significant IHT relief.

In conclusion, protecting your wealth from inflation, currency risks, taxes, and potential estate liabilities is an essential component of comprehensive financial planning. By implementing strategies to address these risks, you can help preserve your wealth and ensure your financial goals are achieved for yourself and future generations.

Chapter 14: Financial Planning for Life's Milestones

Life's milestones often come with significant financial implications, making it essential to plan and prepare for these events. In this chapter, we will discuss financial planning strategies for various milestones, including financing higher education, marriage and family planning, and career changes and entrepreneurship.

14.1 Financing Higher Education

Higher education can be a considerable expense, and planning for this cost is crucial for both students and their families. Some strategies to finance higher education include:

- Saving early: Starting a dedicated savings plan, such as a Junior ISA or a regular savings account, can help accumulate funds for future education expenses.
- Exploring scholarships and grants: Research and apply for scholarships, grants, and bursaries to help reduce the overall cost of higher education.
- Utilising student loans: Government-backed student loans can help cover tuition fees and living expenses, with repayment plans typically based on income after graduation.

14.2 Marriage and Family Planning

The costs associated with marriage and starting a family can add up quickly. To prepare for these expenses, consider the following strategies:

0.1. Establishing a wedding budget: Determine a realistic budget for your wedding and set aside funds to cover the cost, considering factors such as venue, catering, and attire.

0.2. Planning for parental leave: Understand your employer's parental leave policies and how they will impact your income during this period. Consider setting up an emergency fund to cover any additional expenses.

0.3. Saving for future expenses: Establish dedicated savings accounts for anticipated expenses such as childcare, education, or future family vacations.

14.3 Career Changes and Entrepreneurship

Career changes, whether voluntary or due to unforeseen circumstances, can have significant financial implications. Similarly, starting a business requires careful financial planning. Consider these strategies:

- Building an emergency fund: Having a financial cushion in place can help you navigate periods of unemployment or reduced income during a career transition.
- Updating your budget: Reassess your budget to account for changes in income and expenses during a career change or when starting a business.
- Seeking professional advice: Consult with financial advisors, career counsellors, or business mentors to help you make informed decisions and develop a plan for success.

In conclusion, financial planning for life's milestones is an essential aspect of achieving your financial goals and maintaining financial stability. By implementing strategies to save for and manage these significant expenses, you can navigate life's milestones with confidence and enjoy the journey ahead.

Personal Tip: Anticipate and plan for major life events by setting aside dedicated savings and adjusting your financial plan as needed. For example, if you're planning to start a family, consider setting up a dedicated savings account for future education expenses or adjusting your budget to accommodate the additional costs of raising a child.

Chapter 15: Behavioural Finance

Behavioural finance is a field of study that examines the psychological factors influencing investment decisions and their impact on financial markets. This chapter will discuss the main themes in behavioural finance and how they can impact people's investment decisions, supported by relevant statistics and sources.

15.1 Cognitive Biases

Cognitive biases are systematic errors in thinking and decision-making that can affect investment decisions. Some common cognitive biases in investing include:

- Overconfidence: Overestimating one's ability to predict market movements or pick winning investments, which can lead to excessive trading and higher transaction costs.
- Confirmation bias: Seeking and interpreting information that confirms existing beliefs while ignoring conflicting evidence, potentially leading to poor investment choices.
- Loss aversion: The tendency to feel the pain of losses more strongly than the pleasure of gains, which can result in holding onto losing investments for too long or selling winning investments too early.

A study by Barber and Odean found that overconfident investors traded more frequently, reducing their average returns by 1.5% per year compared to more passive investors (source: Barber and Odean, 2000).

15.2 Herd Mentality

Herd mentality refers to the tendency of investors to follow the actions and decisions of other investors, often leading to financial bubbles and crashes. This behaviour can result from a fear of missing out or the belief that the majority must be right. A study by Shiller found that the herd mentality contributed to the dot-com bubble in the late 1990s and the subsequent market crash (source: Shiller, 2000).

15.3 Emotional Investing

Emotions, such as fear and greed, can significantly influence investment decisions, often to the detriment of long-term financial goals. Emotional investing can lead to impulsive decisions, such as buying high and selling low, based on market sentiment rather than rational analysis.

A study by Dalbar found that the average investor underperformed the market by 1.7% per year over 20 years, primarily due to poor market timing and emotional decision-making (source: Dalbar).

15.4 The Impact of Behavioural Finance on Investment Decisions

Understanding the principles of behavioural finance can help investors recognise and manage the psychological factors that influence their investment decisions. Strategies to mitigate the impact of behavioural biases include:

- Developing a long-term investment plan: Establishing clear financial goals and an investment strategy can help investors stay focused during periods of market volatility.
- Diversification: Maintaining a diversified portfolio can help reduce the impact of emotional investing and herd mentality on investment decisions.
- Seeking professional advice: Financial advisors can provide objective guidance and help investors recognise and manage the behavioural factors that may affect their investment decisions.

Personal Tip: Familiarise yourself with common cognitive biases and emotional pitfalls that can impact your investment decisions, and develop strategies to manage them. For example, if you're prone to overconfidence, make a conscious effort to seek out contrary opinions and challenge your own assumptions before making investment decisions.

On the next page is a useful summary table of the main elements of behavioural biases.

In conclusion, behavioural finance offers valuable insights into the psychological factors influencing investment decisions and their impact on financial markets. By understanding these factors and implementing strategies to address them, investors can make more informed decisions and improve their chances of achieving their financial goals.

Behavioural Bias	Description	Impact on Investment Decisions
Overconfidence	Overestimating ones abilities, knowledge, or influence	Excessive trading, underestimating risks
Confirmation bias	Seeking and valuing information that confirms existing beliefs	Ignoring contrary evidence, poor diversification
Loss aversion	A stronger preference fro avoiding losses compared to acquiring gains	Selling winners too soon, holding losers too long
anchoring	Relying too heavily on an initial piece of information when making decisions	Inability to adapt to new information
Herd mentality	Following the actions of others, regardless of one's own knowledge or analysis	Susceptibility to market bubbles and crashes
Mental accounting	Treating money differently depending on it's source, intended use, or location	Sub-optimal asset allocation and spending
Hindsight bias	Believing, after an event has occurred, that it was predictable or inevitable	Overconfidenc e, false sense of skill
Regret aversion	Avoiding decisions that may result in feelings of regret	Inaction, failure to adjust portfolio
Regency bias	Overemphasising the importance of recent events when making decisions	Chasing performance, neglecting long-term trends
Availability bias	Relying on readily available information, rather than a comprehensive analysis, to make decisions	Misjudging probabilities, ignoring less-visible risks
Sunk cost fallacy	Continuing to invest time or resources into a project based on the amount already invested rather than future prospects	Holding onto under-performing investments

Chapter 16: Scams and How to Avoid Them

In this chapter, we will explore the different types of scams targeting UK investors and provide practical advice on how to identify and avoid them. Scams can have devastating financial and emotional consequences, so it's crucial to remain vigilant and stay informed about the latest tactics employed by fraudsters.

16.1 Types of Financial Scams

0.1. Ponzi Schemes: These scams promise high returns with little or no risk by using new investors' money to pay earlier investors. The scheme collapses when there aren't enough new investors to pay existing ones.

0.2. Boiler Room Scams: High-pressure sales tactics are used to sell overpriced or worthless shares, often from unregulated or non-existent companies.

0.3. Clone Firms: Fraudsters impersonate genuine, regulated financial firms to gain your trust and steal your money.

0.4. Phishing: Scammers use emails, texts, or phone calls pretending to be a reputable company to steal personal information, such as login credentials and financial information.

0.5. Pension Scams: Fraudsters target pension savings, offering early access to funds, free pension reviews, or high-return investments that are either high-risk or non-existent.

16.2 Recognising Scams

- Unsolicited contact: Be wary of unexpected phone calls, emails, or texts from unknown sources offering investment opportunities.
- High returns with low risk: If an investment sounds too good to be true, it probably is. Scammers often promise high returns with minimal risk to lure victims.
- Pressure tactics: Scammers may create a sense of urgency, pushing you to make a decision quickly without enough time

for proper research.

- Lack of transparency: Be cautious if a company is unwilling to provide clear and detailed information about their operations or investment offerings.

16.3 How to Protect Yourself

0.1. Verify the legitimacy: Always check the Financial Services Register to confirm that a firm is authorised by the FCA or PRA. Additionally, verify contact details to ensure you're dealing with a genuine firm.

0.2. Be cautious with personal information: Never disclose personal or financial information unless you're confident in the company's legitimacy and security measures.

0.3. Research thoroughly: Investigate investment opportunities, read reviews, and seek opinions from trusted sources before making any decisions.

0.4. Seek professional advice: Consult an independent financial advisor if you're unsure about an investment or need help navigating the financial landscape.

16.4 Reporting Scams

If you suspect that you've encountered a scam, report it to Action Fraud, the UK's national fraud and cybercrime reporting centre. Reporting scams can help protect others and contribute to the fight against fraud. In conclusion, staying informed and vigilant is crucial in protecting yourself from financial scams. By understanding common scam tactics, recognising red flags, and taking proactive steps to safeguard your finances, you can significantly reduce the risk of falling victim to fraud.

Chapter 17: Conclusion

As we reach the end of our journey through financial planning, it is essential to remember that the process does not end here. Instead, successful financial planning requires ongoing maintenance, adaptation, and education. In this final chapter, we will summarise the key themes of the book and provide guidance on maintaining financial discipline, adapting to changing circumstances, and committing to lifelong learning and financial education.

17.1 Maintaining Financial Discipline

Financial discipline is crucial to achieving your financial goals and maintaining a stable financial future. Key aspects of maintaining financial discipline include:

- Regularly reviewing and adjusting your budget to ensure it remains aligned with your financial goals and priorities.
- Sticking to your investment plan, even during periods of market volatility or economic uncertainty, to help ensure long-term success.
- Monitoring your progress towards your financial goals and making adjustments as needed to stay on track.

17.2 Adapting to Changing Circumstances

Life is full of surprises, and your financial plan must be flexible enough to adapt to changing circumstances. Be prepared to reassess and adjust your financial plan in response to major life events or changes in your personal or financial situation. This may include:

- Re-evaluating your financial goals and priorities in response to significant life changes, such as marriage, starting a family, or a career transition.
- Adjusting your investment strategy to account for changes in your risk tolerance or time horizon.
- Reviewing your insurance coverage and estate planning to ensure they remain appropriate for your current needs and circumstances.

17.3 Lifelong Learning and Financial Education

Financial planning is a lifelong process, and ongoing education is crucial for staying informed and making sound financial decisions. Commit to continuous learning by:

- Reading books, articles, and research on personal finance and investing to expand your knowledge and stay up-to-date on industry trends and developments.
- Attending seminars, workshops, or online courses to develop your financial planning skills and knowledge.
- Consulting with financial professionals, such as advisors or planners, to gain insights and guidance on specific financial topics or concerns.

Personal Tip: Commit to lifelong learning and staying informed about changes in the financial landscape. Continuously educate yourself on financial planning topics and seek out new resources to expand your knowledge. For example, consider subscribing to reputable financial publications or attending workshops and seminars to stay current on the latest trends and best practices in financial planning.

In conclusion, financial planning is a dynamic and ongoing process that requires discipline, adaptability, and a commitment to continuous learning. By applying the principles and strategies outlined in this book, you can build a solid foundation for financial success and confidently navigate the complexities of your financial journey. Remember, the key to achieving your financial goals lies in your hands. So stay disciplined, stay informed, and stay focused on your path to financial freedom.

APPENDIX

A. Glossary of Terms

Annuity: A financial product that provides a guaranteed income for life or a specified period, typically used in retirement planning.

Asset Allocation: The process of distributing investments among various asset classes, such as stocks, bonds, and cash, to balance risk and return according to an investor's goals and risk tolerance.

Bonds: Fixed-income securities issued by governments, corporations, or other entities to raise capital. Bondholders receive periodic interest payments and the return of principal at the bond's maturity.

Capital Gains Tax (CGT): A tax levied on the profit made from the sale of an asset, such as stocks, property, or other investments.

Compound Interest: The interest earned not only on the initial principal but also on the accumulated interest from previous periods.

Diversification: The practice of spreading investments across a range of assets or sectors to reduce risk.

Dividends: Payments made by companies to their shareholders, usually from profits or retained earnings.

Enterprise Investment Scheme (EIS): A UK government initiative designed to encourage investment in early-stage, high-risk companies by offering tax relief to investors.

Financial Conduct Authority (FCA): The regulatory body responsible for overseeing financial services firms and protecting consumers in the UK.

Inflation: The rate at which the general price level of goods and services is increasing over time, eroding purchasing power.

Individual Savings Account (ISA): A tax-efficient savings and investment account available to UK residents, allowing them to save or invest money without paying tax on interest, dividends, or capital gains.

Lifetime ISA (LISA): A type of ISA designed to help individuals save for their first home or retirement, offering a government bonus on contributions.

Market Volatility: The degree to which the prices of investments fluctuate over time, often used as a measure of risk.

Pension: A long-term savings plan designed to provide income in retirement, usually comprising contributions from individuals, employers, and the government.

Portfolio Rebalancing: The process of adjusting the allocation of assets in a portfolio to maintain the desired risk-return profile, typically by selling high-performing assets and buying under-performing ones.

Prudential Regulation Authority (PRA): A part of the Bank of England responsible for the prudential regulation and supervision of banks, building societies, and insurance companies in the UK.

Recession: A recession, in simple terms, is a period of negative economic growth that lasts for at least two consecutive quarters, or six months. During a recession, the economy typically experiences a decline in business activity, increased unemployment, and reduced consumer spending.

Risk Tolerance: An individual's willingness and ability to accept the potential losses associated with investing in exchange for the possibility of higher returns.

Robo-advisor: A digital platform that offers automated investment management services, typically using algorithms to construct and manage portfolios based on an investor's risk tolerance and goals.

Self-invested Personal Pension (SIPP): A type of personal pension that provides investors with greater control over their investment choices, allowing them to select from a wider range of assets.

Stocks (Shares): Financial instruments representing ownership in a company. Owning stocks entitles the holder to a share of the company's profits and assets.

Tax Relief: A reduction in the amount of tax owed, often granted by the government to encourage specific types of investment or behaviour.

Venture Capital Trust (VCT): A publicly-listed investment company that provides funding to early-stage, high-risk businesses in exchange for equity. VCT investors can receive tax relief on their investments.

Yield: The income generated by an investment, expressed as a percentage of the investment's price.

B. List of Useful Resources

Financial Conduct Authority (FCA): The regulatory body responsible for overseeing financial services firms and protecting consumers in the UK. The FCA website offers a wealth of information and guidance for investors.
Website: https://www.fca.org.uk/

Prudential Regulation Authority (PRA): A part of the Bank of England responsible for the prudential regulation and supervision of banks, building societies, and insurance companies in the UK.
Website: https://www.bankofengland.co.uk/pra

Action Fraud: The UK's national fraud and cybercrime reporting centre, providing information on the latest scams and advice on how to protect yourself.
Website: https://www.actionfraud.police.uk/

The Money Helper Service: A free, impartial service set up by the UK government, offering guidance on money matters, including budgeting, saving, investing, and retirement planning.
Website: https://www.moneyhelper.org.uk/

The Pensions Advisory Service: A free, impartial service providing information and guidance on pensions, including workplace pensions, personal pensions, and state pensions.
Website: https://www.pensionsadvisoryservice.org.uk/

Pension Wise: A free, impartial government service offering guidance to those aged 50 and over about their pension options.
Website: https://www.pensionwise.gov.uk/

HM Revenue & Customs (HMRC): The UK's tax authority, responsible for collecting taxes, administering tax relief schemes, and providing information on taxation rules and regulations.
Website: https://www.gov.uk/government/organisations/hm-revenue-customs

Financial Ombudsman Service: A free, independent service for resolving disputes between financial services providers and their customers.

Website: https://www.financial-ombudsman.org.uk/

The London Stock Exchange: The UK's primary stock exchange, providing information on listed companies, market data, and investing news.

Website: https://www.londonstockexchange.com/

The Investment Association: A trade body representing UK investment managers, offering industry news, research, and resources for investors.

Website: https://www.theinvestmentassociation.org/

Financial Times: A leading financial news outlet offering in-depth market analysis, investment news, and global economic insights.

Website: https://www.ft.com/

Morningstar: A provider of independent investment research, offering tools and analysis for stocks, mutual funds, ETFs, and other investments.

Website: https://www.morningstar.co.uk/uk/

MoneySavingExpert: A consumer finance website offering tips, tools, and resources on saving money, investing, and personal finance.

Website: https://www.moneysavingexpert.com/

C. Recommended Reading

"The Intelligent Investor" by Benjamin Graham: A classic investment guide that offers timeless advice on value investing and portfolio management.

"A Random Walk Down Wall Street" by Burton G. Malkiel: A comprehensive guide to investing that covers various investment strategies and argues for the efficiency of the market.

"Rich Dad Poor Dad" by Robert T. Kiyosaki: A personal finance book that explores the differences in mindset and financial strategies between the author's "rich dad" and "poor dad."

"The Bogleheads' Guide to Investing" by Taylor Larimore, Mel Lindauer, and Michael LeBoeuf: A practical guide to low-cost, long-term investing inspired by Vanguard founder John C. Bogle.

"The Richest Man in Babylon" by George S. Clason: A collection of parables set in ancient Babylon that teaches timeless lessons on wealth accumulation and financial management.

"Your Money or Your Life" by Vicki Robin and Joe Dominguez: A comprehensive program for transforming one's relationship with money and achieving financial independence.

"The Little Book of Common Sense Investing" by John C. Bogle: A concise guide to low-cost, passive investing strategies that emphasises the importance of low fees and broad diversification.

"The Four Pillars of Investing" by William J. Bernstein: A thorough examination of the key principles that investors should understand to build a successful portfolio.

"The Total Money Makeover" by Dave Ramsey: A step-by-step guide to financial success that covers budgeting, debt reduction, and wealth-building strategies.

"The Millionaire Next Door" by Thomas J. Stanley and William D. Danko: An exploration of the habits and characteristics of America's wealthy, with insights into how they accumulated their wealth.

"The Simple Path to Wealth" by JL Collins: A guide to achieving financial independence and retiring early (FIRE) through simple, low-cost investing strategies.

"The Psychology of Money" by Morgan Housel: An examination of the psychological factors that influence our financial decisions and the importance of developing a healthy relationship with money.

"The Behaviour Gap" by Carl Richards: A look at the common mistakes investors make due to irrational behaviour, and practical advice on how to overcome these pitfalls.

"Nudge: Improving Decisions About Health, Wealth, and Happiness" by Richard H. Thaler and Cass R. Sunstein: An exploration of how "choice architecture" can be used to influence better decision-making in various aspects of life, including personal finance.

"Smarter Investing" by Tim Hale: A practical guide to evidence-based investing, which focuses on building a diversified, low-cost portfolio to achieve long-term financial goals.

Printed in Poland
by Amazon Fulfillment
Poland Sp. z o.o., Wrocław